May your Chosen Path
be forever filled with
happiness. Believe in yourself!

Kira Schiavello

My Chosen Path

A Poetic Reflection of Teenage Emotions

Kira Marie Schiavello

Published by:
BelieveAtlantis Publishing Company
172 Broadway
Woodcliff Lake, NJ 07677

My Chosen Path - A Poetic Reflection of Teenage Emotions
Copyright © 2002-2005 by Kira Marie Schiavello

Photography by Arlene Schiavello

Library of Congress Control Number: 2005905322

ISBN-13: 978-0-9761513-4-0
ISBN-10: 0-9761513-4-0

PRINTED IN THE UNITED STATES OF AMERICA
June 2005

Dedication

Mom, Dad, and Steven, you have always been there for me, and you are all a constant inspiration.

Mom and Dad, you have made me the person I am, and you continue to teach me new things every day.

Steven, you are more than just my little brother, you are my friend. Know that I will always be there for you as I know you will always be there for me.

I thank you for all your patience, and your constant love and support. I will love you always and forever, with all my heart.

Love,
Kira Marie

CONGRESSWOMAN ROUKEMA
SPEAKING TO THE
U.S. HOUSE OF REPRESENTATIVES
ON NOVEMBER 6, 2001

"Mr. Speaker, I rise today to share a poem written by an extremely talented individual, Miss Kira Schiavello of Saddle River, NJ. Kira lives in my district which was particularly hard hit by the World Trade Center disaster. The loss of life and strain on our community has been difficult, to say the least. However, we are finding a new strength in the Fifth District of New Jersey."

"Kira Schiavello has captured the experience of September 11 and the resulting challenges in a moving poem. Kira displayed an eloquence and insight beyond her young years as she not only depicted this terrible tragedy but also expressed the emotional and soul searching reactions of Americans."

"I would like to take this opportunity to share her poem with my colleagues. As we work to protect her generation's future, let us be inspired by the true patriotism and strength that they now show."

**"Mr. Speaker, I ask that the following poem,
written by Kira Schiavello,
be submitted to the Congressional Record."**

"Tragic Tuesday"

*Reprinted in My Chosen Path in memory of the
victims who died on September 11, 2001*

Table of Contents

My Reflections

Reflections

"Decisions" – I often have a difficult time deciding on what the best choice might be in certain situations. Whether about school, family or friends, decisions are a part of every teenager's life, and decision making will change the path of one's life. My poems about "Decisions" are intended to reflect upon some choices that I have made and to encourage others to make right choices.

"Courage" – I believe that courage is lacking in many teenagers today. My poems about "Courage" reflect on an emotion that is not easily achieved, but rather an emotion that one must struggle to maintain. In a world full of peer pressure, it is courage that will distinguish the weak from the strong. It is important to always stay independent-minded, and true to one's convictions.

"**Humor**" ~ I realize that a sense of humor is something that all teenagers need in order to live a happy and full life. Amidst all the stress and the troubles in life, my poems about "**Humor**" hopefully will show others how laughter can make the difference between having a good day or a bad one.

"**Dreams**" ~ It is important for people of all ages to have wishes and goals, especially teenagers. Often the right goals can instill ambition and determination in a person; two important qualities in leading a successful life. My poems about "**Dreams**" emphasize the importance of never giving up, because the only way to succeed is to truly believe.

"**Nature**" ~ Since nature is obviously all around us, it ultimately shapes the lives of all of us. Appreciating nature, and understanding its miracle, will help expand and develop emotions that will produce a more well-rounded person. Hopefully, my poems about "**Nature**" will help teenagers respect and admire nature while increasing their awareness about the negative effects of destroying it.

"Reality" – Some situations in life that could not have been avoided, can still serve as valuable lessons for the future. My poems about **"Reality"** attempt to express the feelings that other teenagers may go through when confronted with the harsh realities of life. Hopefully, teenagers will realize that they are not alone, and their experiences may be used to help make the world a better place.

"Inspiration" – My family continuously encourages me to be the best I can be. Friends and teachers have also helped shape my life since I was a young child. Those that have made a positive difference in a teenager's life should be thanked and not go unnoticed or unappreciated. My poems about **"Inspiration"** acknowledge those that have helped me become the person I am today.

Caution

Caution

These rows of white
Sit patiently between thin blue lines,
Whispering my name.
They beg
To be splotched with my tears,
Creased with my smiles,
Rolled with my laughs.
In consenting, I expose my warm blood
To a deadly chill,
I place my heart in the center of a highway,
I pack my emotions in a foam-filled box,
Ring the doorbell,
And run away.
I reveal myself;
To be judged, to be used against me,
To be misunderstood.
This risk I welcome.
Caution: Contents Fragile.

Decisions

Exchange

You may be one who loves to dream
Of reforming the world's disarray.
But what you first must realize
Is that change can start today.

You have been given this day as a gift
To use as you see fit.
If you believe in what you dream,
To a change you must commit.

Do not think this day is unimportant,
For you are exchanging a day of your being
For the opportunity to improve yourself,
To notice things worth seeing.

By this very time tomorrow
This day will be long past.
In its place is what you leave behind;
Memories that will last.

Do not waste this gift you've got!
Don't leave it on the shelf.
For the changes you wish to see in the world
Can start with you, yourself.

A New Beginning

Midnight, crow whooshed past my window,
Passed and headed for the bare tree, lone,
The winter night chilled to the bone;
The crow's black feathers icy at their tips.

Evil rang the air, a frozen sound,
It stopped the snowflake in its flight,
And encased the darkness of the night;
As midnight perched so oddly bold.

A lapse now noticed in the sinful sound;
A falter, just enough for snow,
Not noticed by the devilish crow;
But faintly falling, nonetheless.

Now midnight saw the dusty white,
And blackness raised its wicked chest,
The crow crowed, crowed at its best;
Yet the snow just came the harder.

Too late, white struck hard like lightening,
Reflecting in midnight's ghastly eyes,
The gentle blizzard ignoring its cries;
Clinging to the nightly black like glue.

Scarcely a crow now, more like dawn,
Shadowed now by a calm of blur;
Destroying the sin of midnight were
These white unsullied slivers of heaven.

Of crow, of night there was none, now,
Resembled dawn, a more saintly dove,
Cleansed by the snowfall that fell from above.
Given a chance, new beginning, accepted.

Dove chirped and fluttered in pride, approval,
And greeted the colors that lit the skies,
Peace, the sweet smell of a silent sunrise;
Its feathers glimmered the whitest white.

Dawn, dove glided past my window,
Passed and landed on the rising sun,
The place where darkness could not run.
The quintessence of evil turned good.

How Beautiful I Look

How beautiful I look,
In shadows and in blush;
How old and how mature;
My lips so red and lush.

But, that reflection is not I,
No, it must be someone else.
For my doll still lies beside me,
My toys upon my shelf.

My days are like a game;
Fun yet such a struggle.
My teddies call for childhood
And I still run to snuggle.

My baby face is covered;
My eyes coated in blues;
Stockings run down my legs
To my dainty high-heeled shoes.

How beautiful I look,
My hair pinned way up high;
Still I know deep in my heart;
That reflection is not I.

Believe

Are you ever too old to believe,
In the wondrous magic around you?
Does your mind get weary of wanting the answers
To the mysteries that surround you?
Haven't you noticed the less faith you have,
The dimmer the fire in your heart?
If you are one of those people
Who doesn't believe;
Maybe it's about time you start.

Life

Life is a disease;
That every person holds.
I've come to see its power
As my own life unfolds.

Some choose to live out life
In sorrow and in pain.
Some lie and injure others,
Some persistently complain.

After seeing loved ones pass away
From the disease that is so rife,
I wished I had been nicer;
And I chose to change my life.

Now I live each and every day,
As if it were my last.
Just like strokes and cancer;
Life can kill so fast!

It is important to remember
To make the best of life's array.
Its existence is so valuable;
Cherish every day.

Expectations

The mind can erupt from the stress,
As the pressure forces its way in.
Expectations interrupt the thoughts,
The destruction begins within.
Anticipation burdens the spirit
Making it harder to achieve.
The weight of any failures
Are impossible to relieve.
Such a major problem
A disappointment can bring;
Too many expectations
Can complex the simplest thing.

Courage

Step by Step

Nothing is so truly sweet
As the pitter-patter of a child's feet,
As it first dares to walk with care
Steps of purity, none compare.
Delicately they thump, thump along,
Footsteps singing their own song
As the child totters, no rhythm or rhyme,
Carefully one step at a time.

Running hard, to the cheering crowd,
Hoping just to make them proud;
Thump, thumping on the mile-long track,
Keep on moving don't look back.
All contenders for the race,
"Come on now, don't lose your pace!"
Pounding persistently, patiently now;
As sweat drips down a tired brow.

Steady steps striking the battleground,
To the beating of a drumming sound;
Proudly they thump, thump all alike,
Freedom humming in every strike.
A victory march of loyalty;
Soldiers, defenders of liberty.
All began with a single stride,
Now marching together, side by side.

Baseball

The little boy dragged his bat
And stepped up to the plate.
He watched the ball come flying by,
And swung a bit too late.

His teammates saw him striking out
And glared at him with blame.
The coach cheered on the losing team;
While he sat alone in shame.

Back at home the child cried,
And wouldn't play again.
The father held him in his arms;
This little boy of ten.

That year the father and his son
Practiced day and night.
The father told him not to quit;
Without putting up a fight.

"You owe it to yourself," he said,
"To give this game your all.
It used to bring you pleasure, son,
This simple game of ball."

"Go back out there and play, my boy,
And get a hit for your dad!
No matter if you win or lose;
You still will make me glad."

The bigger boy went up to bat;
His hat turned to the side.
His dad was cheering from the bench;
His eyes were swelled with pride.

Since the last time he had played;
He must have grown an inch.
For when the ball flew at his bat,
He didn't even flinch.

He swung the bat with all his might,
And hit the ball smack on!
As he rounded past first base,
His coach yelled, "That one is gone!"

Because he hit that perfect shot,
His team took home the win;
But what he remembered from that day,
Was the joy he felt within.

His teammates gathered in a crowd;
But to his dad he ran;
He slapped him five, up high and low,
And hugged his biggest fan.

"You did it son, I knew you could,
That ball was surely flying.
You just had to still believe,
And never give up trying."

Truth in a Sea of Lies

Deep in the forest, protected by the trees,
I've hidden, as the leaves block out the world.
Clinging to branches that hang down low;
True to myself, but greedy as can be,
For I won't share my truth with the sea of lies;
Although it might catch on and change the tide.

I fear the lies will blind my virgin eyes,
And bring me the world I wish not to see.
Shattering the serenity I know so well;
Like a rock skipped on a glassy pond,
The ripples relentless and infinite it seems.
Some moving away, some reaching to me.

But, I must show the world;
I must stand strong,
Anchored in the sand I have got to stay;
For the only other choice is to conform,
And I'd rather not be the dark sky at night,
But instead the stars that shine for the world to see;
Shining with truth and individuality.

I will teach all the darkness to twinkle with us stars,
Rather than staying a lie in the crowd.
I'll teach them to always be sincere to their souls;
And to live through honesty, not lies.
I've always wished for more stars in the night;
When one day the whole world will shine bright.

The Masses

Stop trying to determine who I am
by the photocopied robots you see in the halls.
Don't compare me
to that plastered image on the magazine covers,
or that perfect look on TV.
I am none of those things.

Don't liken me to those liars,
those backstabbers, those hypocrites,
that love you when they're down,
leave you in their glory.
Their standards will never again
dictate who I am,
Nor will they tell me who I am not.

I've finished my game of tug-of-war;
I've dropped the rope
and they've tumbled over like dominoes.
The masses are no longer my worst enemy,
They're what I've overcome.

Courage

An iron-gray mountain staggers high;
Concealed in snow and perilous in its way.
All other plights it does defy,
Ice-capped peaks reach to the sky,
No rules does it obey.

Up above, the forest white,
Where wildlife does abound;
Stays undiscovered in its might,
Without the courage to lose sight,
Of the dull and droning ground.

Such courage does often cower,
For it is not the trees that sway to and fro;
Nor trees that through storms loom and tower,
It is instead the fragile flower;
That opens in the snow.

Humor

Laughter

How I love to see you laugh,
How like stars your eyes do twinkle;
How your happy smile widens,
And your face begins to crinkle.

How your smile lights up the world,
Like the sun on an August day;
How your grin lifts the spirit,
And puts all worries away.

How your laughter is pure,
Not fake but from the heart;
How your giggles are contagious,
And make me want to start.

How your joy you love to share,
With every frowning face;
If everyone laughed as you did,
All hatred would erase.

My Journey

Yesterday I walked the streets,
Moseying along in my cold bare feet.
The gravel made indents in my heels,
My toes were numb and hard to feel.

Today a red carpet covers the ground,
I can walk alone without a sound.
The velvet soothes my tired soles,
As I walk on, the next day unfolds.

Tomorrow I'll travel along the beach,
I'll walk where the waves are just out of reach;
I'll let my feet sink in the sand,
Buried deep down in the land;
I'll cool them off with a dip in the sea,
Oh how happy my feet will be.

Backwards Day

What if there were a Backwards Day,
That happened once a year?
If you wanted to go forward in your car,
Would you put the shift in rear?

Would you smile when you're feeling down,
Or cry when feeling glad?
If someone else were nice to you,
Would you instead get mad?

Would you wear your clothes all inside out,
And walk backwards if you could?
Or if someone tucked you in at night,
Would you say instead, "Night good"?

Oil and Vinegar

Oil and vinegar just don't mix;
It's a fact of life you simply can't fix.
It's like trying to suck an ocean dry,
Or count every star that's in the sky.

The sun and the moon just won't obey,
Neither will shine in one place a whole day.
It's like trying to whistle an offbeat tune,
Or using a cotton ball to pop a balloon.

One plus one will never make three;
No matter how many times you wish it to be.
It's like trying to make an ice cube sink,
Or surviving a year without a drink.

Oil and vinegar just don't mix;
It's a fact of life you simply can't fix.
Although you may like to deceive them;
They're facts of life – you must believe them.

Paint

Upon all the people who hide their true selves,
With my red paint, a fine coat will be placed.
Now they may be whatever they please,
For their identity is truly erased.

Each time they act just like all the others,
I'll give them a purple dot.
They will do anything just to fit in,
Whether they agree with it or not.

Many have this polka-dotted disease,
Although they may not know.
For it takes confidence and originality
To let one's true self show.

If you find yourself a disbeliever,
Just look around and see.
You are surrounded by people in purple and red,
Including you and me.

Dreams

Devotion

When I think of you...
I think of stars in the sky;
Of snowflakes that fall from way up high.
Of sun rays that pierce a cloudy day;
Of happiness that never fades away.
Of the soft, warm sand along the ocean;
Of my love for you and of my devotion.

When I think of you...
I think of tall palm trees;
Of a hot summer's day cooled by a soft breeze;
Of puffy clouds like cotton balls,
Of the vibrant colors observed in the fall.
Of children laughing, girls and boys;
Of all the things that bring me joy.

Christmastime

The little girl sat in front of the window;
On a stool clothed in white silk.
Next to her lie cookies,
And a glass of ice-cold milk.

On her feet she rested;
Her toes poking out behind her.
The wooden door was shut,
So nobody could find her.

The lights were very dim;
So she could see her star.
She gazed at it reflectively
As it glistened from afar.

She did not wish for clothes;
Or for money or for toys.
She wished Santa would bring happiness,
To all the girls and boys.

She wished for love and peace;
That everyone could share.
She wanted to end hatred,
And teach people to care.

She was not being impractical;
As she wished to end all crime.
She knew anything was possible,
When it was Christmastime.

Dusty Dreams

Truth
Time and again ignored
Existence
In shadows of fear
Hardly a life, barely living
My dreams
Pressed out of my thoughts

Curled in a corner's darkness
Cobwebs
Creeping in my mind
A mind unused and grown old
As I seek an illusion of safety

My dreams
My destiny
Shining so bright, nearly blinding
Dreams buried so long
Too long!
Now covered in dust and uncertainty

Only I can struggle to stand
To dig my dreams from their grave
The first step
No matter what size
Is one step closer to defeating
My doubts

Subtle Signs

I think I touched you,
Though you stood ten feet away.
I think I felt your heart quiver
Beneath my gaze,
As my gaze touched yours...
Or maybe that was my own beat.
I think I saw your eyes smiling
In the quiet dark.
I know it was no accident,
Your smiling eyes in the quiet dark,
Your playful nudge,
The gentle warmth of your palm on my back,
The subtle signs when no one was watching;
When witnesses were blinded by the night.
I wonder, would they have noticed in the light?
Maybe It was only my insides that thundered.
I think I touched you then.
I think you felt it and knew it was right,
That acknowledgement of affection
From ten feet away.
Still, for the sake of your shy heart,
Let's pretend no one's ever watching.

Soul's Symphony

I press each key so gently;
My hands tiptoeing across the piano,
A featherlike sound dances in the air.
The song builds intensity;
As more passion strikes each note.
The strings vibrating fervently,
Pleading for more --
And I will gladly give it,
To hear chords unite in perfect harmony.
It's just the piano and me now.
My entire body leaning into the beauty of the music.
My soul wrapped up in paradise.

Dreams

In dreams there are no rules;
In dreams there are no lies.
In dreams there is always happiness,
In dreams there are no cries.

As the night turns into day,
You start to think it through.
Why can't these dreams be reality?
Why can't these dreams be true?

Nature

In the Forest

Here in the forest;
The trees hover like giants.
Crisp leaves settle on the ground,
Twitching in the invisible breeze.
Branches sway;
Reaching their stems
High to the quarter moon,
As a child would reach
Its arms lovingly to its mother.
Treetops shield wildlife
From the abyss above.
Here in the forest;
All is peaceful.

Snowflakes

The sun lowers in the sky;
The wind picks up its pace.
Snowflakes fall from way up high
Then settle into place.
Children catch them on their tongues,
They melt without a trace.
Hours, minutes, seconds later;
A white blanket covers Earth's face.

L'île aux Fleurs

L'île est très colorée,
Il y a beaucoup de fleurs.
Il est le paradis des plantes;
Et il fait chaud toujours.
Il y a des arbres immenses;
Ils sont si verte toute l'année.
Sur les belles plâges,
On peut se bronzer.
Il y a des forêts tropicales,
Et des incroyables jardins.
Il y a une grande chute d'eau,
Comme une montagne.
Le sable est comme or;
Il est très beau;
Quand on voit la mer bleue;
Déjà on est amoreaux.

A World Without Deceit

Atop the world I lie,
Peering down at day and night,
Only peace and splendor are visible;
Animosity is hidden from sight.

The void around me is endless;
The silence seizes my mind.
The Earth is a blur of beauty,
So wonderful and kind.

The peaking snowcapped mountains
Are so small and delicate.
Below me the ocean twinkles,
And rests in each inlet.

Tiny specs are traveling
Across each threadlike street.
The world is so delightful
When it's absent of deceit.

Meadow

Here in the meadow;
Lush green grass leaps from the ground.
Flowers bloom;
Dew drops clinging to their delicate petals,
And absorbing the sun's mighty rays.

Butterflies brush each flower's face,
Camouflaged in the vibrant bouquet.
They soar free,
As the wind lifts them;
And releases them with care.

Here in the meadow;
Each plant is enriched with life;
Life brought by intense heat
And freezing rain.
And each is surrendered
To the infinite powers of nature.

Raindrops

Raindrops glistened on the black pavement;
Like stars in the midnight sky.
Somewhere a good soul suffered,
And made the heavens cry.
Fire red leaves shivered in the cold breeze
And shuddered from the silver rain.
With sadness pouring from above;
They felt the angels' pain.

Raindrops shimmered on the snaking sidewalk;
Like the blinding light of the sun.
Somewhere a good soul flourished,
And requested loads of fun.
Tears of joy came from the clouds
As they witnessed the great event.
To every animal and every plant;
Joy and love was sent.

Sunrise

The sun smears its colors;
Pinks, oranges and reds.
Over the rumbling turquoise ocean,
Its soothing beauty spreads.
Beyond the clear horizon;
The night turns into day.
Creatures of every shape and kind
Breathe in the colorful bouquet.
The sunlight warms the world;
And embraces it with care.
Its rays are innocent and pure;
A gift for all to share.
Emotions are relinquished
To the quickly rising sun.
The view is gone in seconds;
Another day has begun.

Reality

My Biggest Fear

My biggest fear surrounds me;
I can't see it, but I know it's there.
I hold it back, yet it still comes;
In the black night I can almost feel it,
But it never concedes to show its face.

My fear glimmers during tragedy,
In my delicately dripping tears.
For it knows the sorrow that seems inescapable
Will soon be yesterday, then last week,
And then long gone among the years.

My fear leaps when I laugh,
Along my happy giggles.
Laughing in my face it seems;
That my joy will shortly be a faded memory;
Another tiresome, "Back in my day…"

My fear is in the dusty gray locks
That will one day lie on my pale pillow;
In the baby face I'll surely lose,
And in all the creases in my life,
That will valiantly appear on my skin.

My fear follows me as I play
In the playgrounds in the park,
Which, before long, will no longer welcome me back.
My fear is time; yes; each tick of a clock,
Unrelenting and infinite;
Like nothing else in the world.

Kira Marie Schiavello   69

Sweet Revenge

Today is the big day!
You can smell the sweet revenge.
You've tried everything you could;
And chose to take avenge.

You've packed extra in your bag;
As you travel off to school;
It's their fault anyway,
For calling you a fool.

Well it's second period now;
Yes, it's time to start the plan.
You warned them from the start;
When the teasing all began.

On the second floor;
Shrill shots ring down the hall.
Bleeding fingers point at you;
You take no time to stall.

You dash out of the school;
And are caught by the police.
Struggling to escape;
Their grip will not release.

And now you sit alone;
On a bed that's stiff and hard.
Your profile forever tainted;
Your life forever scarred.

Ah, what sweet revenge.
Now five live never more.
Their families cry in terror;
Their bodies coat the floor.

So was the choice a good one?
Are you proud of what you've done?
You've taken life from others;
With five shots out of a gun.

There were so many other choices!
Why did you fail to see?
Someone would have listened;
Of this I guarantee.

A teacher or a counselor,
Would have gladly offered aid.
So much could have been done;
To avoid this fatal crusade.

You caused death to end your loneliness;
But still alone you stay.
Your selfishness caused only harm,
Destruction, and dismay.

War

My dearest loving parents,
This is not what I had planned.
We were told to get this over with;
It was the President's demand.

We gathered arms in daylight,
And set out from the base.
The folks there were so friendly,
Not an enemy to face.

The children taught us songs,
The parents thanked us too;
Was it just an act,
Or were they being true?

My friends and I, we laughed,
We thought that we were right.
That war was not that bad,
Until it turned to night.

In darkness they all came,
Invisible to see;
We shot into the blackness,
My newfound friends and me.

As dawn rose from behind us,
I looked around to find,
My best friend on the ground in pain;
Death may have been more kind.

His face was almost gone,
His eyes looked so afraid,
I bandaged up his bloody wounds
And ran to get him aid.

He screamed in piercing agony,
A voice from his hollow head,
I held his hand for hours,
Until my best friend was dead.

My friends and I still fight,
To make up for what was done;
But I am no longer human,
Just a robot with a gun.

I hope it will be over soon,
But doubts are growing now.
With your picture in my pocket,
I'll fight to live somehow.

Have faith in my returning home,
As soon as this war is done.
You know I'll always love you both,
Till then, Your Loving Son.

Was It Worth It?

Before you left your mom and dad,
    You swore you would not drink.
No one would make you, if you said no,
    Or at least you did not think.
    You could just skip the party,
    But then you'd miss the fun.
A lot of people would be drinking,
    But, of course, not everyone.

When you arrived at the celebration,
    Your methods proved untrue.
All the guests were drunk and partying;
    All the guests; but you.
    Sure, you wanted to leave,
    But then they all would laugh;
They'd tease you and make fun of you,
    And drink more on your behalf.

Instead, you decided to stay,
    And save yourself from shame;
If the rest were caught for drinking,
    You still were not to blame.
    This choice was a mistake,
As were the careless ones before it;
    In your heart, you knew this,
    But chose just to ignore it.

The minutes passed by slowly,
Till the drunk ones went insane;
They held the liquor to your face
And threatened you with pain.
They proceeded, then, to beat you,
Forcing toxins down your throat;
They left you passed out on the lawn
And fled somewhere to gloat.

You found yourself in a stiff white bed
With doctors and nurses around you;
You heard your parents sigh with relief,
How lucky that they found you!
You knew you held a partial blame,
Although you'd kept your vow;
You could see it in your parents' eyes
And felt the guilt somehow.

In time, you would recover
From every physical ache;
But the damage done inside you,
Time could never shake.
In spite of feelings of regret,
You never could reverse it;
One night had changed your entire life –
Was it really worth it?

Her Message

My best friend had cancer.
It was a horrifying thing.
Every day I'd visit her,
With all the hope I could bring.

She was the greatest person I knew;
She was pretty, and smart.
And despite all her troubles,
She kept her good heart.

At the thought of my friend,
My eyes start to blur.
For the day that she died;
It was just me and her.

"My friend," she had said,
"I don't want to die;
I try not to believe it,
But I'd be living a lie."

"I don't want to leave
All those I love so upset.
They mean so much to me;
So this message they must get."

"Please thank all the people
Who brought me their toys.
Give courage to those suffering;
Those brave girls and boys."

"Tell Mom that I love her,
And the same to Dad too.
For they're everything to me;
And taught me everything I knew."

"Tell my sis she's my idol;
And she always will be.
I pray that she's given
Better luck than me."

"And to you, my dear friend,
You were there when in need.
Take my love and good luck;
I know you'll succeed."

"My most important message
Goes out to all.
Live life to its fullest,
And always stand tall."

"Be kind to your loved ones;
Don't dwell on the past.
You must seize every day;
'Cause it could be your last."

Then she closed her hollow eyes,
And squeezed my hand tight.
And I hugged her goodbye,
As she joined with the light.

My Song

I often look back on my days of childhood
And smile at tender memories.
It's certainly been awhile
Since I've captured fireflies
And marveled at their pulsating glow,
Or spent hours
Uncontrollably rolling down a grassy hill.
I long for those days when I could fly,
Propelled only by a father's knees.
Days when my spirit soared like the kite
Trailing behind my tiny footprints.

So much has changed since then,
Since the jump rope rhymes and silly tunes.
Childhood spirit seems masked with age,
Society smothers the sweet belly laugh
Still tickling inside; trapped, suffocating.
I suppose it's just another scene
In all the life that stretches before me.
One big race for acceptance
A stampede of clones and empty minds
As soaring young spirits
Dive like the kite that once flew high.

I can't say that childhood tickling will ever leave.
No doubt it will remain until my bones
Begin to bend under my weighted soul,
Dying to spread its wings once more.
That is, unless I choose to let it free,
To take me to my place within the ticks of time.

Maybe this way, even the grayness of my hair
Will not disguise the child
Eternally lingering within.
Grayness, which shall never label me old,
Rather only show I've lived long,
Had time enough to sing my song;
I only hope my song will be worth singing.

Tragic Tuesday

On September 11, 2001,
America was under attack.
There was an empty gap in NYC,
And the skies above were black.

First, the North Twin Tower was hit,
By a hi-jacked, passenger jet.
The sight of the explosion in the sky,
Americans will never forget.

Then, to the world's shock and disbelief,
The South Twin Tower was crashed into.
Those close by just ran and screamed;
It was like nothing they had ever been through.

As if nothing else could go wrong,
Two more planes were seized!
They hit Pennsylvania and The Pentagon,
Until finally the terrorists were pleased.

But the damage to the US was not done,
For the Twin Towers dropped to the ground.
Blinding dust filled up the air;
And the world shook with the trembling sound.

Under the ruble, five stories high,
Are brothers, sisters, dads and moms.
Their innocent lives are gone forever;
Because of the terrorists' flying bombs.

America has never seen a tragedy,
As devastating as this.
It will continue to affect our everyday lives,
For as long as we exist.

The faceless criminals were looking to ruin,
Our happiness, our liberty, and our spirit.
But surely they were stunned to find;
That they came nowhere near it.

If those evil cowards were here today;
They'd see people sob and cry.
But behind those tears, they'd surely find,
Our flag still flying high.

In the face of this Tragic Tuesday;
America did unite.
And those who tried to hurt our pride;
America will fight.

We'll join as one and win the war,
Till our strength is doubted no longer.
If anything, this tragedy
Will only make us stronger.

Inspiration

To my teachers...

A door is opened to a world of opportunities,
A child embarks on a journey within.
A teacher makes these miracles possible;
With compassion they help the adventure begin.

To enrich a fertile mind with knowledge,
A teacher must teach from the heart.
It is this special kind of love
That sets givers and takers apart.

The success of a teacher is endless;
For all teachers were once taught by one.
Everyday awaits another miracle;
A giver's job is never done.

Teachers deserve appreciation
For all the things they do.
To the teachers who opened new doors for me;
I am thanking you.

To my best friends...

I cannot even begin to thank you
For all the things you've done.
It is so rare to find true friendship like ours,
And our story together has just begun.

I turn to you when I need aid;
Or when I'm simply feeling blue.
Whatever the conflict I am in;
Somehow, you always get me through.

You've taught me more than you can know,
Through all the decisions you've helped make.
You are beautiful people, inside and out,
And advice from you I will always take.

I can count on you for support and a smile;
For encouragement, understanding, and care.
To your honesty, kindness, and sense of humor;
No other friend could ever compare.

Your personalities are special in so many ways;
You are each truly one of a kind.
The countless memories we have shared,
Will never leave my mind.

To my mom...

Ever since I was a baby,
You helped to guide me,
Every step of the way.
All your time spent teaching me,
To know right and wrong;
Has made me who I am today.

I don't know how you do it,
How you're always there,
Putting our needs forever first;
Trying hard to make us smile,
In any way you can,
Even when we're at our worst.

And yet you still find time,
For us to talk together;
Sharing concerns and views.
You'll gladly offer encouragement,
And advice from the heart;
That I never can refuse.

A glimpse of your beautiful smile,
Will brighten gloomy skies,
And sweep away my fears.
Your loving personality,
And your gentle hand,
Will wipe away my tears.

I admire your genuine beauty.
Not only on the outside;
But on the inside as well.
You are honest, kind,
Understanding, and supportive;
And you inspire me to excel.

I always want to make you proud,
You're my best friend ever;
Mom, you know it's true.
You've helped me grow
Through thick and thin,
I'm so lucky to have you.

To my dad...

From the moment I entered the world,
You cradled me with care.
You made me laugh and fed me,
Though I was unaware.

I quickly learned to speak;
Dada was your name.
My giggles were contagious
When we would play a game.

Older and older I got,
I learned to read and write;
Still we would play airplane,
And I'd be shrieking with delight.

Still, today, you guide me,
Through bad times and through good.
I've overcome them with your help,
You always knew I could.

I could not ask any more from you,
You're the very best dad ever;
I hope to grow up just like you,
So very kind and clever.

Thank you for being my hero,
It's a very special title.
You've made me who I am today;
You'll always be my idol.

To my peers...

Your *future* is always built on your past.

Look at the trees that surround us. From the outside they look tall and strong, ready to face any storms that should come their way. But cut open any one of those tree trunks and examine their core. In the core of that tree you will see a ring for every year the tree has been growing. If there was a rainy season, you will find a thick, dark ring marking that year. If the weather was dry one season, a warped and small ring will show the spot.

Just as those trees carry their past with them, we carry our memories with us. On the outside, we may brave whatever new experiences come our way, but on the *inside*, our core shows that we, too, have rings of good and bad; rings of our time spent as teenagers. However you or I may wish to treat that time, *our teenage years are a part of us, and always will be.* It is our responsibility to use *yesterday* to make the most of tomorrow.

We just need to look around to see some of the most important parts of our past.

Look at your family. At first, we see moms and dads that made us do chores and set unreasonable curfews. We see brothers and sisters that teased us relentlessly and got us in trouble... but look closer and we see the people that have always believed in us, even when we may have doubted ourselves. They're the ones who have helped build our character, character that influences every decision we make and determines the kind of people we are.

Even if we may now be ready to continue on to the next stage of our chosen path, *as I'm sure many of us are*, our families may not be ready to let us go. We owe them so much, so hug your family members and thank them for being there for you.

Now look at your teachers. Teachers that made learning exciting, and even teachers that you may have felt were out to get you by making sure you spent your entire weekend doing homework. They have *all* challenged us to stretch our minds, personally seeing that we reached our potential.

When our chosen path brings us into the real world of college or careers, to what knowledge do you think you are going to turn? Maybe you will *never* have to solve an algebra problem again, but I'm talking about the knowledge of *decision-making, analyzing, problem solving.* Just try imagining a life without these skills. So don't forget to tell your teachers how much they are appreciated.

Finally, look at your peers. The *greatest* treasure of our past resides in the hearts of our closest friends and classmates. We have cheered *together*, we have laughed *together*, and we have cried *together*, and somehow, when it felt like our worlds were collapsing, *together* we emerged even stronger than before.

We are all in this together; *we are* the future! Look at the responsibility we have on our shoulders! *Society* will depend on us, our *children* will need us, someday even our *parents* will rely on us. When we look back on our teenage years, we will know that, *together,* we have helped define the path we will follow for the rest of our lives.

In the future, our lives will be filled with great friends we've yet to meet, experiences we've yet to dream, and harder work than we've ever imagined. Cherish your past forever, and don't be afraid to use this past to help make the next path of your life's journey, *the best one yet.*

Discover something!
Invent a product!
Raise a child!
Volunteer!
Be a leader!
Create a masterpiece!

Let your voice impact the *world*, the *future*, the *core* of another person!

And be sure that for *every* year to come and for every path you choose, the rings in *your* core are stronger than the last.

My Chosen Path

So Much to Offer

You have so much to offer,
So much to give,
So many opportunities,
Such a reason to live.

Believe in yourself;
In your uniqueness and strength.
Stretch your possibilities
To their maximum length.

Always be positive,
And aim your goals high.
Discover your talents
And reach for the sky.

Realize your dreams;
Do not let them defray.
Determine tomorrow
By your choices today.

My Chosen Path

During my journey through life,
I came to a fork in the road.
The trail to the left ran straight,
Its erosion thoroughly showed.
Its hills were small and worn,
It was obviously the easier way;
Others would choose this track quickly;
But the decision caused me delay.

I approached the difficult choice,
Joined by hundreds more,
They chose the path to the left;
The one always chosen before.
The right path led to a forest
Thick with jagged rocks and trees.
The unforgiving conditions
Would force most to their knees.

Beyond each trail's horizon,
The destination was unknown.
Yet I continued to the right,
And traveled on alone.
I chose the route with pride;
Like few others in the past;
Just by risking doing so,
The others I surpassed.

I dared to be different.
I let myself stick out.
Despite obstacles along the way,
In my abilities I had no doubt.
I paved my own path to victory
Just by reaching for the best.
I chose to trust my potential;
Upon my own request.

About the Author

Kira wrote these inspirational poems while attending Ramsey High School from which she graduated as valedictorian. Although she is now studying engineering at Princeton University, she has published these poems in their original form to reflect her emotions as a young teenager.

Kira lives in Saddle River, NJ with her Mom, Dad, Brother, and German Shepherd. Some of Kira's interests, besides her passion for writing poetry, include spending time with family and friends, sailing, reading, tennis, playing piano, and studying sign language. Kira was Executive Editor of her high school's newspaper and is now on the staff of a campus magazine at Princeton. She also serves on the Engineering Council, and is Vice Chair of her Residential College.

The inspiration for Kira's poems came from her family and friends, as well as from works by other poets. In writing this book, she hopes that other teenagers, their siblings, and their parents, can better relate to the wide range of teenage emotions, and be motivated to choose the right path in life.